HEALED GOD'S WAY

HEALED GOD'S WAY

God can heal you by changing your lifestyle
according to His biblical principles.

How to win the battle against cancer, how to overcome anxiety and depression, and how to succeed
in everything, God's way.

(Recipes included)

Brigida Tellez

Dedication

I dedicate this book to my children Elani & Erick
for being my inspiration, and my parents Luis
Rafael and Carmen for their emotional support and
because I owe them everything I am, also for their
teachings and their words of encouragement.
To my dear friend and sister Carolyn, who left
this world too early and fought with all her soul
to conquer cancer; this book is to honor you
my sister and friend. I also want to dedicate this
book for what we were not able to do for others
together. I hope God allows me to help other
women and men affected with this illness.

Acknowledgments

First of all I want to thank God immensely for using me to help others and for giving us the salvation through His son, Jesus, who was sacrificed on the cross for us.

Thanks to my daughter, Elani, whom God used to revise and edit this book, and to Pastor Wilma Zalabak for the final revision.

Also, many thanks to Mr. Kerry Pharr, host of "In Your Corner" ministries, broadcast by Daystar Television Network, whom God put in my path. Due to his expertise in the area of publications, he inspired me to finish this project and accomplish my dream of writing my own book.

To my husband Edmond and his mother, for their help during my illness, Lydia, who came as an angel to take care of my family and me during my illness, Niriam and her children, Clarita and Tiola. Also, to

Pastor Tirado, Maylor and Dr. Graham, Aida, Waleska, and all the members of their church for their support and ceaseless prayers, and to two friends that never stop helping me with their delicious meals and continuous prayers, Gladys and Chela.

Finally, thanks to the group of Maximized Living with Dr. Fred Roberto, his wife Kimberly, and Dr. Melissa Sells, who were introduced to me by Dr. Fran E. White. With them, I have learned that God comes first, then eating properly, detoxifying, exercising the body and mind, and releasing stress from the nervous system are all vital steps to staying healthy.

Foreword

This book, written with love to glorify the name of God and for love of the neighbor, is a collection of information and data, carefully extracted from the Bible, the Word of God, from other publications, and my own experience with God in my life and as a survivor of breast cancer.

With this book I want only to show and demonstrate that God has always been with all His children, because He loves us and even though sometimes we don't realize it, He always takes care of us. God healed me not only from cancer and anxiety, but also from other diseases, but the greatest thing is that, through these tests, God taught me to change to new habits in my life, which have been handy, written and explained biblically.

I would also like to make it clear that I am not a professional in medicine, or nutrition, nor do I intend to change the living habits of anybody. My intention is simply to inform and help others in a simple and easy way, and to demonstrate that all of this, through my experience has worked so far. I am a witness to this and I believe it by faith because it is the way of God.

On the topics that I have written here, much has been published, but the majority of people have not paid attention, and they are not aware of the important principles that can improve their lives. Also, each person and each author has his or her own point of view in this regard.

I am just a human being touched by God, and it is my duty to say through my experiences, that God continues to be the doctor of doctors. Here, I also explain how we can succeed in every area of our lives, if we trust Him.

Table of Contents

Acknowledgments · · · · · · · · · · · · · · · ·vii

Foreword · ix

Chapter 1 The way to find the truth
and experience miracles · · · · · · · · · · · 1

Chapter 2 How God can heal you by changing
your lifestyle according to His
biblical principles
(mind, body and spirit) · · · · · · · · · · · · 4

Chapter 3 How to overcome anxiety,
God's way · · · · · · · · · · · · · · · · · · 27

Chapter 4 How to overcome
depression, God's way · · · · · · · · · · · 36

Chapter 5 How to be healed through
nutrition, God's way. · · · · · · · · · · · · 42

Chapter 6 The food in biblical times
and what may have been
eaten by our Lord Jesus · · · · · · · · · · 54

Chapter 7   My recipes and menus for the week ·· 75

Breakfast · 77

Lunch · 85

Dinner · 91

References · · · · · · · · · · · · · · · · · · · 101

About The Author · · · · · · · · · · · · · 103

1

The way to find the truth and experience miracles

Jeremiah 33:6 _⁶ Behold, I will bring it health and healing; I will heal them and reveal to them the abundance of peace and truth._

In other words, and relating to the title of this book, "Healed God's Way," I want to start off by explaining how all of us are able to be healed from any disease by ourselves, by changing bad habits in our lives for good ones and succeeding in everything we do, according to the will of God, if we simply obey His biblical principles.

When I say, "according to His will," I make it clear that whatever we ask in our prayers to God must be preceded by an "agreement to His will" because not all that we ask for is always the best for us, even if we think it is, we should consider whether it will really be good for us, according to the will of God.

> **Joshua 1: 8** - *This Book of the Law shall not depart from your mouth, but you shall meditate in it day and night, that you may observe to do according to all that is written in it. For then you will make your way prosperous, and then you will have good success.*

First off, I want to recount events to show that our Lord Jesus came more than 2,000 years ago and still, even though we don't see it, He continues doing miracles according to His will and therefore, if we believe in Him, we can be certain that He will heal us of any illness or anything wrong (either physical or mental).

In 1996, while still living in Venezuela, I was offered by the company I used to work with, to be transferred to the office in the capital of Venezuela: Caracas, after a few years of working with them as a Civil Engineer on projects for an oil industry in Puerto La Cruz, the coastal area in Venezuela. I refused the offer and decided that it was time (after 12 years of career in my profession) to seek another direction in my life, so I prepared everything to come to the United States of America, leaving my beloved parents, my siblings, my friends, and with that, my whole life of 36 years living there.

When I first came to the US, one of the first people I contacted was my current husband, which put me in contact with an engineering company that hired me. I thanked God, as it was the first miracle I experienced. The company immediately sponsored me for my permanent residency, and later gave me the privilege of becoming a citizen of the United States of America.

After many years of prayers, God blessed me with another miracle. I got married after a long bachelorhood, and a couple of years later, God blessed me by letting me become the mother of a beautiful little girl, and in a few more years, a precious boy.

Together, we lived as a family with personal and spiritual challenges, but with the main goal of bringing all our family and the people around us to true Christianity, keeping us in the faith of Jesus as our Savior and obediently following the Ten Commandments of God.

2

How God can heal you by changing your lifestyle according to His biblical principles (mind, body and spirit)

3 John 1: 2 - *Beloved, I pray that you may prosper in all things and be in health, just as your soul prospers.*

If God sees in us that we need to be molded in His way, we need to make drastic changes, or God will allow something tough and painful to happen to us in order to change and clean our lives. Sometimes God allows difficult and painful situations into our lives for the better. If we want to be changed for our own good, then we have to be thankful that God—as a good father—takes us into account.

"To get rid of the old and shape the new, it requires an arduous process." (Max Lucado, *On the Anvil*–Spanish Version *"En el Yunque"*, 59-60).

1 Peter 1: 6-7 - [6] *In this you greatly rejoice, though now for a little while, if need be, you have been grieved by various trials, [7] that the genuineness of your faith, being much more precious than gold that perishes, though it is tested by fire, may be found to praise, honor, and glory at the revelation of Jesus Christ.*

Thanks to God, who allowed me to go through one of the toughest tests that one can go through in life, so that my faith could be strengthened. My lifestyle changed completely, and although it is a little hard to say, I thank God for the painful moments we went through as a family; it happened to perfect us and glorify the name of Jesus, the Son of God.

On February 17, 2011, I was diagnosed with breast cancer. Figuratively, the world came over me. It was a shock to everyone around me. I never thought something like this would happen to me. I had been taking care of myself by eating well, not smoking, not drinking alcohol, or sodas (soft drinks). I had never heard that someone among the women of the family had been diagnosed with cancer before. Anyway, it was a terrible experience, but the fact that I was not going to be there for my children was killing me more than the disease itself.

All my life I had been super healthy! Then suddenly, the difficult decision to lose my breasts, and later, after double mastectomy surgery, receiving the news that I needed to receive chemotherapy treatment, ended up tearing my heart and I became disappointed with God.

I wondered and cried out at the same time: "Why to me? What did I do? What did I eat? or What didn't I do? I believed in you Lord! I had taken care of myself so much, I've had faith!" Then, I changed my question to, "What for my Lord?"

The days were passing and I didn't see or hear the Lord's voice. I decided to surrender to Him everyday, to put my problem in His hands and thank Him for everything that was happening, even though I was not able to understand it, without imagining what His great purpose would be.

I also asked myself, "Does He not love me?" because every time I visited doctors and hospitals during those long and endless days in this very difficult time, the only things I got were more and more bad news about my case.

However, the one who was telling me that He didn't love me was God's enemy, which in essence is the one who puts those lies in your mind. Later, in Chapter 3, I explain how to handle these feelings with success, God's way, during the process of diseases and pain, which cause depression and anxiety.

Among the things that began to show His compassion for me was when finally, God put a mark on my body and in my heart that never would erase, in order for me to not forget that He really loves me, and loves you too, because we all are His children, and what father will not love their children?!

Luke 11: 10-13 - [10] *For everyone who asks receives, and he who seeks finds, and to him who knocks it will be opened.* [11] *If a son asks for bread from any father among you, will he give him a stone? Or if he asks for a fish, will he give him a serpent instead of a fish?* [12] *Or if he asks for an egg, will he offer him a scorpion?* [13] *If you then, being evil, know how to give good gifts to your children, how much more will your heavenly Father give the Holy Spirit to those who ask Him!"*

At the end of one of my chemotherapy sessions, I got a burn between my arm and my right hand (see photo). The pink mark left on me that day, which I still carry in a heart shape, was similar to a little stamp I got while praying for an answer from the Lord, with these words written as follows: "You are a Treasure to God." This was the answer from our Lord.

He again showed me He loved me and that He had a wonderful plan for my life, for my family, and for those around me, but at that time, I was not able to visualize it.

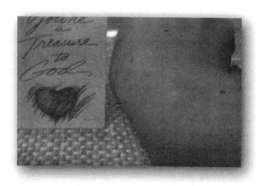

To calm my desperation and my nerves and to try to clear my mind to make the decisions I had to make, I began to ask God to give me patience, wisdom, to increase my faith, to wait for His plan, and to understand everything that was happening to me.

Hebrews 6:12 - *that you do not become sluggish, but imitate those who through faith and patience inherit the promises.*

Romans 10:17 - *So then faith comes by hearing, and hearing by the word of God.*

James 1: 2-5 - *[2] My brethren, count it all joy when you fall into various trials, [3] knowing that the testing of your faith produces patience. [4] But let patience have its perfect work, that you may be perfect and complete, lacking nothing. [5] If any of you lacks wisdom, let him ask of God, who gives to all liberally and without reproach, and it will be given to him.*

What the enemy wants the most is to break you down, crush you down and for you to abandon or give up on your dreams, but if during the tribulation and adversity, you do not let yourself become overwhelmed, your faith will be strengthened and will become powerful.

God created us perfect, and therefore He can (God is Almighty) correct or can fix any damage in or on us, but even with God being perfect and we, being created in His own image, the disobedience has led us to sin and consequently we contract diseases and attract failures in our lives.

Genesis 1:27 - *So God created man in His own image; in the image of God He created him; male and female He created them.*

9

I learned to let it go, day by day, and especially to thank God without even knowing how the end of the nightmare I was living would turn out, and how the unwrapping of the whole process of this disease would be.

I had to run into many obstacles and many tests to understand that God loves me and that if I did not learn the simple way (searching His Word) I had to learn the hard way (getting sick or going through pain) then maybe it would be the way to stop doing what I was doing wrong with my life.

My advice is to not wait to go through a difficult situation to make changes in your life.

What was I doing with my life, that God does not want me or you to do?

1 Corinthians 6:19 - *Or do you not know that your body is the temple of the Holy Spirit who is in you, whom you have from God, and you are not your own?*

Most of the diseases that afflict humanity are the result of their own wrong habits: some for ignorance, and others for not searching in the book of life that has been supplied to us by our God. His word is in the Bible and because of the rush we live in, we do not sit quietly to search and find His laws and the truth that is for the benefit of us all.

It is not possible to glorify God while living in violation of His laws that are the laws of the lives of all human beings on earth.

"A sick body or a sick mind also suffering from a disordered life, are impossible to be sanctified." (Ellen G. White, *Consejos sobre la Alimentación*, 50- In English: *Counsels on Diet and Foods*).

"A healthy body allows God to work in us to perfect and achieve success in our Christian life." (Ellen G. White, *Consejos sobre la Alimentación*, 51-In English: *Counsels on Diet and Foods*).

After many mistakes in how I was treating my body, which is the temple of the Holy Spirit, God showed me the right way. Below I list some of the mistakes we make and submit to our body that we should avoid:

1. **Lack of rest**. It is important that adults sleep at least eight hours and children about 9-10 hours. Depriving ourselves of sleep causes significant and irreparable harm; during the hours of sleep is when our bodies and damaged cells in our body are repaired to the point that if we do not sleep enough, this

repair process is interrupted and then following diseases occur. We also need to go to bed early and get up early. Apart from that, we have one day a week that God gave us to rest, and it is one of His Commandments meaning that after a week of work, we should rest one day and dedicate it to God to praise Him. This gives much peace and health to our soul, mind, and body. My family and I enjoy it to the fullest, and we feel an immense joy when that day comes.

Mark 1:35 - Now in the morning, having risen a long while before daylight, He went out and departed to a solitary place; and there He prayed.

Exodus 20: 8-11 - 8"Remember the Sabbath day, to keep it holy. 9Six days you shall labor and do all your work, 10but the seventh day is the Sabbath of the Lord your God. In it you shall do no work: you, nor your son, nor your daughter, nor your male servant, nor your female servant, nor your cattle, nor your stranger who is within your gates. 11For in six days the Lord made the heavens and the earth, the sea, and all that is in them, and rested the seventh day. Therefore the Lord blessed the Sabbath day and hallowed it.

The Sabbath, as God's Commandments mention (Exodus 20:8), is equivalent to Saturday (New King James Version, NKJV).

Many people lose their health by abandoning this principle: "The Sabbath rest does the same as sleeping: Allows the body and mind relax, unwind and recover" (Don Colbert, *The Seven Pillars of Health*, 61).

2. **Living under stress.** We should not stress or worry in excess. I mean, everyday, life has its own stress but we should not let anything (such as money), and no one (negative and destructive people) rob us of our peace. When hard times arise, that stress robs us of much of our lives. Our immune system, which protects us from illness and keeps us strong against the attacks of the environment and daily living, is greatly affected and at risk, hence we must not allow added stress to our body. In conclusion, worry does not solve anything. We must put all our problems in God's hands and He will take care of and solve them in His way, which

is the best for us, His children; therefore, God gives us the release of those loads.

> **Psalms** *55:22 - Cast your burden on the Lord, and He shall sustain you; He shall never permit the righteous to be moved.*

> **Matthew** *11:28 - Come to Me, all you who labor and are heavy laden, and I will give you rest.*

3. **Eating what is not food**. The foods that God created for our daily consumption were not processed, nor do they come in boxes. Boxed foods are transformed to be more durable in the markets for sale and consumption in mass or bulk, with a countless number of chemicals that are really bad for our health. In the past, the food consumed was completely fresh and natural; it was not treated with hormones to increase the volume and meet the demand, as they are nowadays with pesticides and antibiotics so that the crops do not get damaged or consumed by animals and other organisms. Today, big food companies,

in order to not lose money, and earn more, apply all these kinds of harmful and toxic procedures to put our health in risk. We were not created to eat meat from other animals; that was not the original plan of God for us, His children, neither that all vegetarians should eat soy, especially the highly toxic soy produced in this country, nor the gluten of wheat flour that is genetically modified, bleached, and processed, having no nutrients for our body. It will intoxicate us and we will end up sick. We should not consume refined sugar, and much less artificial sweeteners. We have grown into a global culture in which everything must be sweetened. God created a vast variety of vegetables, fruits, and seeds with their natural sweetness, that apart from providing health and energy, detoxify us and we can enjoy a long and pleasant life.

In Chapter 5, I emphasize and extend over this issue about how our diets should be, God's way.

4. **Lack of forgiveness**. Forgiveness is very important. Do not hold any resentment in your heart, not with anyone nor with yourself; let it out and it will set you free.

James 4:12 - *There is one Lawgiver, who is able to save and to destroy. Who are you to judge another?*

Ephesians 4:32 - *And be kind to one another, tenderhearted, forgiving one another, even as God in Christ forgave you.*

Proverbs 3: 7-8 - *⁷ Do not be wise in your own eyes; fear the Lord and depart from evil. ⁸ It will be health to your flesh, and strength to your bones.*

5. **Lack of joy.** Laugh and cry when you feel like it! I do it often, and it feels good! This sets you free from the burdens within your body and relaxes you by letting the stress out.

   James 1: 2-4 - *² My brethren, count it all joy when you fall into various trials, ³knowing that the testing of your faith produces patience. ⁴ But let patience have its perfect work, that you may be perfect and complete, lacking nothing.*

Proverbs *15:15 - All the days of the afflicted are evil, but he who is of a merry heart has a continual feast.*

Proverbs *17:22 - A merry heart does good, like medicine, but a broken spirit dries the bones.*

6. **Lack of physical activity.** Not exercising or remaining sedentary is terrible for your health. Exercise refreshes your body, renews your energy, and gives you strength. It is very important to get exercise routines, to get up to stretch our bodies and release the trapped nerves and toxins accumulated in our bodies, and thus one starts with more energy to face the challenges of the day. The benefits of exercise are (Don Colbert MD, *The Seven Pillars of Health*, 119-126):

    - Preventing cancer
    - Preventing heart attacks and heart disease
    - Improving system flow of lymph nodes
    - Reducing tension or stress
    - Promoting weight loss and reducing appetite

- Preventing diabetes by controlling blood sugar
- Increasing perspiration to release toxins through the skin and getting rid of the accumulated waste in our body
- Decreasing the aging process
- Strengthening bones
- Improving digestion and regulating the frequency of bowel movements
- Providing a recovered sleep
- Reducing anxiety and depression
- Improved memory
- Increased energy:

  When I finished my chemotherapy treatment, I was extremely weak. I remember that I was not able to walk even to the mailbox outside the house, but I started to take more and more steps, first in the street in front of our house from end to end, and by the following year, I was walking faster until I got to walk marathons consisting of over twenty miles a day, and I did not feel tired anymore.
- And many more benefits

Regular exercise also produces cardiovascular activity that helps your heart release energy to burn calories, and at the same time lose weight, also reducing high and bad cholesterol, and causing new cells to regenerate daily. The amount of exercise your body requires can be from a minimum of 15 minutes daily. Being inside the home or driving in a car, most of the time, is a mistake. You have to go out at least for a walk and get some sun and fresh air. It is better do this early, or at least do other physical activities and be in contact with the nature that God created. In the past, and in Jesus' times, there were no cars, so if you observe their ages, they used to last longer because people of that time were more active and used to walk everywhere. These walks were hundreds of miles: "The way our Lord Jesus used to exercise in this land was walking" (Don Colbert MD, *¿Qué comería Jesús?*, 172—In English: *What would Jesus eat?*). Another example that exercise is vital is that of my grandfather Don Tito Téllez, musician and conductor of the Band of the State of Carabobo in Venezuela, from the years 1955-1974, who used to walk a lot and everywhere. He used to tell us that he never drove a car, and was never really sick. Just when he was 104 years old, he fell down from a rocking chair and after that fall, he never recovered and passed away in the year 1996.

7. **Lack of adequate water intake (dehydration).** Our body is composed of approximately 70% water. Water is the most important nutrient for our bodies. Some even believe it is related to the cure of many diseases. Without water, the organs in our body do not function properly. Also remember that through perspiration, urination, and defecation, the water in our bodies is lost. Water plays a vital role in regulating body temperature and transporting nutrients and oxygen to our cells. Water also helps with detoxification; in other words, water cleans impurities from our bodies. The water we use to drink and bathe in should always be lukewarm, preferably filtered, alkaline, and clean. Also, if one waits until one gets thirsty, most likely one is dehydrated. Among the many benefits of water, it helps you lose weight and helps improve memory. An estimate of the amount of water that we must drink is:

½ of your body weight in ounces of water.

Example: If I weigh 155 Lbs. => ½ x 155 = 77.5/8oz (cup) => I should approximately drink 9 cups (each 8 ounces) of water daily.

8. **Lack of adequate air.** How I like to breathe the air, and even better if it is pure! Today there are very few places in the world, I would say, almost nowhere, where the air is pure and uncontaminated. However, instead of being inside the home, I get out early to breathe the morning air: "The influence of pure and fresh air makes the blood flow healthily throughout the body, tends to strengthen the body, while at the same time its influence is felt defined in the mind, for imparting a degree of composure and serenity, excites the appetite, and makes digestion more perfect, inducing a healthy and sweet sleep" (Ellen G. White, *Consejos sobre la Alimentación, 123–In English: Counsels on Diet and Foods*).

9. **Lack of sunlight.** The sun gives us energy, which is very important for our health. By exposing your bare skin to sunlight daily, your body loads with energy, and your blood cells benefit. Sunlight is a major source of vitamin

D production in humans. This vitamin combats daytime sleepiness, reduces symptoms of depression, strengthens muscles, helps to absorb calcium essential for bones, reduces the chance of asthma, and reduces the likelihood of cancer, such as breast, colon, prostate and lung. In fact, when I was in a naturist hospital with a group of people, with a desire to heal myself naturally before my surgeries, they took blood samples of everyone with the result that the only ones who had low levels of vitamin D were those suffering from cancer. Unbelievable, but true!

Scientists have shown that exposing your bare skin to sunlight at noon is better for your health, even if sunscreens are not used, because it is the time of the day when the ultraviolet light reaches its peak in the spectrum. Sunscreens contain more toxic components likely to cause skin cancer. Ideally, researchers say, to expose your bare skin to sunlight while unprotected around 12:00 noon for about 10-15 minutes depending on the location of the land where you live and your skin tone. I usually expose my skin to sunlight at least 10 minutes a day, if possible on my lunch break, whether it be at home or at work.

My recommendation is that if you are not able to regularly expose your bare skin to sunlight, then you should take vitamin D_3 supplements instead of D_2. This is because when ultraviolet light from the sun strikes the skin, humans synthesize vitamin D_3, so it is the most "natural" form. Human beings do not make vitamin D_2 (A. Moyad, Mark. "Vitamin D: A Rapid Review." *Medscape*. WebMD LLC, 2015. Web. 14 July 2015).

10. **Lack of doing fasting**. Fasting is abstaining from all or some kinds of food or drink, and going through a period of time in which your body is purified to consecrate to God in prayer. This practice also helps us to detoxify. Fasting is important because it helps us build our character to surrender to God and to have temperance, which is self-control in our attitudes and desires, especially our appetite, our minds and emotions, and of our flesh. Fasting can submit our spirit to God completely so that God can use us for His purposes. Fasting is also another practice for healing, God's way.

> *Joel* 2:12 - *"Now, therefore," says the Lord, "Turn to Me with all your heart,*

with fasting, with weeping, and with mourning."

The following advices are found in the book of Ellen G. White, *Counsels on Diet and Foods,* page 51:

- "Indulging in eating too frequently, and in too large quantities, over-taxes the digestive organs, and produces a feverish state of the system. The blood becomes impure, and then diseases of various kinds occur. A physician is sent for, who prescribes some drug which gives present relief, but which does not cure the disease. It may change the form of disease, but the real evil is increased ten-fold. Nature was doing her best to rid the system of an accumulation of impurities and could she have been left to herself, aided by the common blessings of Heaven, such as pure air, and pure water, a speedy and safe cure would have been effected."

- "The sufferers in such cases can do for themselves that which others can not do as well for them. They should commence to relieve nature of the load they have forced upon her. They should remove the cause. Fast a short time, and give the stomach chance for rest. Reduce the feverish state of the system by a careful and understanding application of water. These efforts will help nature in her struggles to free the system of impurities."

- "There are some who would be benefited more by abstinence from food for a day or two every week than by any amount of treatment or medical advice. To fast one day a week would be of incalculable benefit to them."

All the ten mistakes mentioned above should be avoided, for consideration and respect for our body. These issues are like fashion; everyone is talking and reading about it. Here, I only named and briefly explained what is necessary for knowledge, and as a living testimony of the damage caused by carelessness in obeying these principles given by God that still stand today. Later in the future, if God's will allows it, I will write another publication in more detail about each of them, or maybe I'll talk more and give lectures related to these health issues. In addition, my cookbook is almost done. In Chapter 7, I include some of my recipes. God gave me the gift of creativity to design buildings, houses, pipelines systems, and roads among others as an engineer. As I worked in building my own home, God helped me build my character when I accepted Him in my heart as my Savior. Even in the tribulation from this disease, I learned to create delicious and healthy meals.

> **Psalm** *34:19 - Many are the afflictions of the righteous, but the Lord delivers him out of them all.*

All tribulations in our lives show us the love of God, to make us perfect in Him!

> **Psalms** *46:1-3   God is our refuge and strength, a very present help in trouble. [2] Therefore we will not fear, even though the earth be removed, and though the mountains be carried into the midst of the sea; [3] Though its waters roar and be troubled, though the mountains shake with its swelling.*

3

How to overcome anxiety, God's way

Philippians 4: 6-7: [6] *"Be anxious for nothing, but in everything by prayer and supplication, with thanksgiving, let your requests be made known to God;* [7] *and the peace of God, which surpasses all understanding, will guard your hearts and minds through Christ Jesus."*

If God tells us not to be anxious, He is promising us that we are worrying for "no reason," however, our nature is to be concerned and worry, without taking into account the stress these worries cause us, but if we stop instead and read, meditate, think, and believe in His word, then we should not worry. Putting our burdens in God's hands frees us from troubles because we are trusting in Him. Not trusting in Him is denying that He exists.

Here in this chapter, I explain how, by my own experience, one can control and learn to handle these harmful and unnecessary feelings if we learn to trust in our God, and also by removing certain habits from our daily lives.

It is easy to say it, but now let's put it into practice, God's way!

The most noticeable symptoms when you have anxiety are:

1. Fear
2. Nervousness
3. Trembling and sweaty hands and body
4. Extreme preoccupation with or without reason
5. Agitation
6. Pressure in the chest by excessive tension
7. Light headedness, which produces a feeling that you're going to lose your mind
8. Shortness of breath
9. Constant thoughts, usually negative
10. Panic attacks

All of these symptoms are generated for several reasons, mostly by excessive stress, or this same stress accumulated by some event that has happened in our lives that we have not solved, we have not overcome it, or we have not forgiven, which caused or causes us pain. They also may be caused by a poor diet, for example, with excess of sugar and flour, as also of processed foods, chemicals that alter our nervous system, lack of rest, consumption of soft drinks, alcohol, smoking and caffeine, not sleeping the necessary hours required by our body to rest and recover the energy spent by the daily work, and finally the lack of exercise.

My daily routine, first thing in the morning if possible, is to meditate on the word of God or just talk to God (pray), fasting preferably, if weather permitting, outside in contact with nature, without shoes I put my feet on the grass and deeply breathe the air in the morning. This relaxes me, and thus my body is cleaner and my mind is clearer to hear His voice. Then I drink a glass of natural water, preferably with lime or lemon, or a natural herb (chamomile, linden, or others) tea. Then after exercise, I have a smoothie with fruits, vegetables, and nuts (almonds are the best because they contain protein), and take a vitamin B complex supplement. To do this ritual, it is necessary to wake up and be out of bed early.

Something that helps me a lot is singing and praising God, and writing; I pour out any feelings, and I make plans to eliminate anything that may be causing me fear: a disease, of losing a job, or that I don't have the money for this or that. Thinking too much about the past or the future doesn't help at all and solves nothing.

Then, watching the anxiety from that perspective, we must not waste our time and much less our health. Remember that God loves us and that any situation that we are facing should be focused on His promises. We should always think that any situation, even the most painful one, happens for a reason, although we may not understand it. God will not allow us to live it if there is not a purpose behind it.

My advice is that when facing fears, they will fade away and weaken.

Similar to how the giant Goliath in the Bible was confronted by David, I also try to face my fears, especially the monster that scares immensely, as I like to call, "anxiety." There are many other monsters in the world: debts, disasters, divorce, deceit, diseases, and depression, among others. These threats, as monsters, walk around us stealing our sleep, peace, and joy. Once you know the footsteps of your Goliath, his disturbing words, his deceptions, whether it be of debts that you can not pay, of some dramatic and harmful people who steal your tranquility, of those who scoff you for your falls and your flaws, faults, or sins that you can not forget, and the uncertain future that torments you, similar to David, we can also face our giant, even if you do not consider yourself strong, exceptionally gifted, intelligent, or equipped with the best or the most holy, we must do and learn what David did. He faced his monster, Goliath, by focusing on God. The same God who helped David will help you if you are ready and willing to do the same.

The most powerful prescription is in the Bible, which is the word of God. It is free and available to everyone.

Here are some biblical quotations related to fear:

Isaiah 41:10 - *Fear not, for I am with you; be not dismayed, for I am your God. I will strengthen you, yes, I will help you, I will uphold you with My righteous right hand.*

Isaiah 41:13 - *For I, the Lord your God, will hold your right hand, saying to you, 'Fear not, I will help you.'*

Isaiah 51:12 *"I, even I, am He who comforts you. Who are you that you should be afraid of a* man who will die, and of the son of a man who will be made like grass?

Psalms 56:11 - In God I have put my trust; I will not be afraid. What can man do to me?

Psalms 56:3-4 - [3] Whenever I am afraid, I will trust in You. [4] In God (I will praise His word), In God I have put my trust; I will not fear. What can flesh do to me?

Psalms 27:1 - The Lord is my light and my salvation; whom shall I fear? The Lord is the strength of my life; of whom shall I be afraid?

1 John 4:18 - There is no fear in love; but perfect love casts out fear, because fear involves torment. But he who fears has not been made perfect in love.

Proverbs 3:24-26 - When you lie down, you will not be afraid; yes, you will lie down and your sleep will be sweet. [25] Do not be afraid of sudden terror, nor of trouble from the wicked when it comes; [26] For the Lord will be your *confidence, and will keep your foot from being caught.*

1 Peter 5:7 - *throwing all your anxiety on Him, for He cares for you.*

Psalm 34:4 - *I sought the Lord, and He heard me, and delivered me from all my fears.*

John 14:27 - *Peace I leave with you, My peace I give to you; not as the world gives do I give to you. Let not your heart be troubled, neither let it be afraid.*

The enemy of God, that I prefer not to utter his name (that's why you may have noticed throughout this book that I do not regard him), is responsible for putting fear into us, putting bad thoughts of any kind, and even the unthinkable (thoughts that are clearly not of us and much less of God), to make us feel guilty, but his evil nature wants us, the children of God, to be distressed and anxious, and in addition, he wants to steal our peace. At that time is when we have to muster up courage and boldness, and discard any mental attack. Take these verses as a shield against such attacks:

Deuteronomy *31:6 - Be strong and of good courage, do not fear nor be afraid of them; for the Lord your God, He is the One who goes with you. He will not leave you nor forsake you."*

Taking into account that our God is love, safe in His love, we will be freed from fear.

1 John 4:8 - *He who does not love does not know God, for God is love.*

Put your fear in His hands of mercy and put that burden on the Lord; He will do the work to give us rest and to rid us of that discomfort, called anxiety, caused by these absurd fears in our minds, that if we have full confidence in God, and we do not pay attention to it because we are clear that these are lies of the enemy of God, then these fears, little by little, will fade away and they will not be part of our lives. When problems and difficult situations come to us, or if we simply feel anxious without any reason, we will effectively handle those feelings, to such an extent that they will not be so strong because we will have put total trust in the Lord, Who will liberate us from this evil feeling, and we will be healed, God's way.

"Depression, anxiety and panic attacks are not signs of weakness. They are signs of trying to stay strong for a long time" (*Anonymous*).

The times I tried to seek help from psychologists or psychiatrists, I was never healed completely with their help and medicines, with all my respect for professionals, nothing nor no one but ourselves and God, our Creator, knows our hearts and minds.

One of three of us go through this at least once in our lives; therefore do not feel bad about being or having experienced these symptoms. I have lived it and I have overcome it with the help of my only psychologist and friend, our Lord Jesus, God's way.

4

How to overcome depression, God's way

In this chapter, I will explain some key points on how we can overcome depression, God's way.

Depression is a condition that causes discouragement and sadness in a person, either because of some deficiency in the body, for situations of health, disease, unemployment, heartbreak, divorce, death of a loved one, frustrations, disabilities, abuse, physical deformities, sin, shame, and even issues pertaining to racism and ethnicity. Some medications, used for anesthesia in surgery, can also cause depression, and so can many other things that cause one to not concentrate and have a normal life or live in peace. In some cases, the person sadly ends up taking his or her own life.

You are not alone in your feelings. Great men of faith, and giants of the Bible, felt discouraged (Mark

Finley, *Estudiando Juntos, 101*–In English:*"Studying Together"*).

This usually happens when we do not have confidence or joy, due to putting God aside. Internally, we possibly grew up with low self esteems, or other situations in our lives could be the cause. There are also imbalances in the metabolism of our bodies because of our poor or unhealthy diets. Medications can also cause it. A typical example of depression due to drugs is after a surgery, or after childbirth, due to the medicines used for anesthesia, which produce some degree of depression or hormonal imbalance in our system. Another example can also be when women are pregnant, at puberty, or in the process of menopause.

When you simply do not know the profound love God has for us, and if we are away from the truth that is handy in the Word of God, God's enemy attacks us in this weakness and takes advantage to the fullest to destroy us.

If Jesus, the Son of God, gave His life for us, He would not have given His life for nothing. We have an immense value in the eyes of God, even if we sin.

John 3:16 - *For God so loved the world that He gave His only begotten Son, that whoever* believes in Him should not perish but have everlasting life.

God, our loving Creator, brought us to the world to live in abundance in every way if we obediently and joyfully surrender our lives to Him.

Things that God allows to happen in our lives are because He has a good plan for our lives of development, progress, and prosperity as human beings.

Jeremiah 1: 5 - "Before I formed you in the womb I knew you; before you were born I sanctified you; I ordained you a prophet to the nations."

Jeremiah 29:11 - For I know the thoughts that I think toward you, says the Lord, thoughts of peace and not of evil, to give you a future and a hope.

Isaiah 43:18 - Do not remember the former things, nor consider the things of old.

Isaiah 43:25 - I, even I, am He who blots out your transgressions for My own sake; and I will not remember your sins.

2 Corinthians 5:17 - *Therefore if anyone is in Christ, he is a new creation; old things has passed away; behold, all things have become new.*

Do not let your emotions control you. It's easy to say, but by focusing our eyes on Jesus Christ, the Son of God, we must not forget, that for any obstacle that prevents us from living in peace or that causes us pain or discomfort, for any difficult or painful situation, we have the biggest and most powerful God Who is bigger than any obstacle that prevents us from being happy and having peace. God sent His Son to set us free of all destructive feelings. Never forget that everything in this world, even things created by God, is transient or temporary. We have the hope of His promises.

Hebrews 10: 16-17 - [16] *"This is the covenant that I will make with them after those days, says the Lord: I will put My laws into their hearts, and in their minds I will write them,"* [17] *then He adds, "Their sins and their lawless deeds I will remember no more."*

Philippians 3: 13-14 - [13] *Brethren, I do not count myself to have apprehended; but one thing I do, forgetting those things which are behind and reaching forward to those things which are ahead, [14] I press toward the goal for the prize of the upward call of God in Christ Jesus.*

Hebrews 6:12 - *[12] that you do not become sluggish, but imitate those who through faith and patience inherit the promises.*

Hebrews 10: 35-36 – *[35] Therefore do not cast away your confidence, which has great reward. [36] For you have need of endurance, so that after you have done the will of God, you may receive the promise.*

We need to clearly have in mind that those feelings are lies of the enemy of God, and all that he wants is to keep us unhappy, anxious, nervous, pessimistic, frustrated, insecure, guilty, lonely, sad, and with many other negative and destructive feelings to produce depression in us.

John 16:20 - *Most assuredly, I say to you that you will weep and lament, but the world will rejoice; and you will be sorrowful, but your sorrow will be turned into joy.*

Indeed, Jesus said His disciples would experience great sadness, which would then be turned to joy.

Even if your father, or your mother, or both have left you alone or abandoned, we have the Father of all that will never abandon us and we shall not want:

Psalms 23:1 - *A Psalm of David. The LORD is my shepherd; I shall not want.*

Psalms 27:10 - *When my father and my mother forsake me, then the Lord will take care of me.*

5

How to be healed through nutrition, God's way.

3 John 1: 2 - *Beloved, I pray that you may prosper in all things and be in health, just as your soul prospers.*

God wants us to prosper and be in good health! In this chapter, I will go deeper into nutrition, because during these years of being cancer free, thanks to the mercy of God, our Lord, is the area where he has been perfecting me, and He has taught me the importance of why we should care for our bodies that are the temple of the Holy Spirit.

1 Corinthians 6: 19-20 - *[19] Or do you not know that your body is the temple of the Holy Spirit who is in you, whom you have from God, and you are not your own? [20] For you were bought at a price; therefore glorify God in your body and in your spirit, which are God's.*

God created everything good. In Genesis 1, throughout the entire chapter, the word "good" appears seven times, but even still, with everything being good, what God created with love to feed us, nowadays, we have to be careful, especially with the variety of fruits and vegetables that are being polluted by man on this earth, especially with the air and the soil pollution which increases the toxic load on our bodies whenever we consume the products that grow in it.

Genesis 1: 31 - *Then God saw everything that He had made, and indeed it was very good. So the evening and the morning were the sixth day.*

Although everything God created was good, remember that after Adam and Eve sinned in the beginning, everything received the taint of sin.

For those who do not want to follow a vegetarian diet, God created some animals for specific functions on this earth, therefore not all meat from animals must be for human consumption.

The original plan of God for man was that we were to be vegetarians, same with the rest of the creatures created by Him.

> **Genesis 1: 29-31** - [29] *And God said, "See, I have given you every herb that yields seed which is on the face of all the earth, and every tree whose fruit yields seed; to you it shall be for food. [30] Also, to every beast of the earth, to every bird of the air, and to everything that creeps on the earth, in which there is life, I have given every green herb for food"; and it was so. [31] Then God saw everything that He had made, and indeed it was very good. So the evening and the morning were the sixth day.*

We can clearly see how the original diet was when God created us and how the maintenance of His creation would be.

However, most importantly, we must obey God Who created us, and generally, whoever creates anything also creates the rules, as they are the ones who designed the creation, so everything will work out well accordingly.

In the six hundredth year of Noah's life, came the flood, and as there was rain for forty days and forty nights, God obliterated every living thing that was on the face of the earth. Then, things changed because God saw that humanity was sinning.

> **Genesis 7:23** - [23] *So He destroyed all living things which were on the face of the ground: both man and cattle, creeping thing and bird of the air. They were destroyed from the earth. Only Noah and those who were with him in the ark remained alive.*

> **Genesis 9: 3-4** - [3] *Every moving thing that lives shall be food for you. I have given you all things, even as the green herbs. [4] But you shall not eat flesh with its life, that is, its blood.*

Well, "all" did not mean we could eat snakes, rats, crocodiles, horses, or pigs, for example. God had indicated earlier to Noah that there were clean animals that were good for us to eat, and unclean animals, which God does not allow for us to eat. Our God clarified that later in chapter 11 of Leviticus and Deuteronomy 14, when about a thousand years after the time of Noah, the story of Moses appears, where God gives instructions about food related to clean animals (pure) and unclean animals (impure). All of God's laws related to health were given to us with love so that we do not become sick and so that we can live a full and happy life.

Many doctors and scientists today have discovered that the paths of God, with obedience and respect, are the best to reduce disease in humanity.

Leviticus 11: 1-23, 29-30, 41-47 - ¹*Now the Lord spoke to Moses and Aaron, saying to them,* ² *"Speak to the children of Israel, saying, 'These are the animals which you may eat among all the animals that are on the earth:* ³ *Among the animals, whatever divides the hoof, having cloven hooves and chewing the cud—that you may eat.* ⁴ *Nevertheless these you shall not eat among those that chew the cud or those that have cloven hooves: the camel, because it chews the cud but does not have cloven hooves, is unclean to you;* ⁵ *the rock hyrax, because it chews the cud but does not have cloven hooves, is unclean to you;* ⁶ *the hare, because it chews the cud but does not have cloven hooves, is unclean to you;* ⁷ *and the swine, though it divides the hoof, having cloven hooves, yet does not chew the cud, is unclean to you.* ⁸ *Their flesh you shall not eat, and their carcasses you shall not touch. They are unclean to you.*

⁹ 'These you may eat of all that are in the water: whatever in the water has fins and scales, whether in the seas or in the rivers—that you may eat. ¹⁰ But all in the seas or in the rivers that do not have fins and scales, all that move in the water or any living thing which is in the water, they are an abomination to you. ¹¹ They shall be an abomination to you; you shall not eat their flesh, but you shall regard their carcasses as an abomination. ¹² Whatever in the water does not have fins or scales—that shall be an abomination to you.

¹³ 'And these you shall regard as an abomination among the birds; they shall not be eaten, they are an abomination: the eagle, the vulture, the buzzard, ¹⁴ the kite, and the falcon after its kind; ¹⁵ every raven after its kind, ¹⁶ the ostrich, the short-eared owl, the sea gull, and the hawk after its kind; ¹⁷ the little owl, the fisher owl, and the screech owl; ¹⁸ the white owl, the jackdaw, and the carrion vulture; ¹⁹ the stork, the heron after its kind, the hoopoe, and the bat. ²⁰ 'All flying insects that creep on all fours shall be an abomination to you. ²¹ Yet these you may eat of every flying insect that creeps on all fours: those which have jointed legs above their feet with

which to leap on the earth. ²² These you may eat: the locust after its kind, the destroying locust after its kind, the cricket after its kind, and the grasshopper after its kind. ²³ But all other flying insects which have four feet shall be an abomination to you.

²⁹ 'These also shall be unclean to you among the creeping things that creep on the earth: the mole, the mouse, and the large lizard after its kind; ³⁰ the gecko, the monitor lizard, the sand reptile, the sand lizard, and the chameleon.

⁴¹ 'And every creeping thing that creeps on the earth shall be an abomination. It shall not be eaten. ⁴² Whatever crawls on its belly, whatever goes on all fours, or whatever has many feet among all creeping things that creep on the earth—these you shall not eat, for they are an abomination. ⁴³ You shall not make yourselves abominable with any creeping thing that creeps; nor shall you make yourselves unclean with them, lest you be defiled by them. ⁴⁴ For I am the Lord your God. You shall therefore consecrate yourselves, and you shall be holy; for I am holy. Neither shall you defile yourselves with any creeping thing that creeps on the earth. ⁴⁵ For I am the Lord who brings you up out of

the land of Egypt, to be your God. You shall therefore be holy, for I am holy. ⁴⁶ 'This is the law of the animals and the birds and every living creature that moves in the waters, and of every creature that creeps on the earth, ⁴⁷ to distinguish between the unclean and the clean, and between the animal that may be eaten and the animal that may not be eaten.

Deuteronomy 14:3-21 (Clean and unclean meat) ³ "You shall not eat any detestable thing. ⁴ These are the animals which you may eat: the ox, the sheep, the goat, ⁵ the deer, the gazelle, the roe deer, the wild goat, the mountain goat, the antelope, and the mountain sheep. ⁶ And you may eat every animal with cloven hooves, having the hoof split into two parts, and that chews the cud, among the animals. ⁷ Nevertheless, of those that chew the cud or have cloven hooves, you shall not eat, such as these: the camel, the hare, and the rock hyrax; for they chew the cud but do not have cloven hooves; they are unclean for you. ⁸ Also the swine is unclean for you, because it has cloven hooves, yet does not chew the cud; you shall not eat their flesh or touch their dead carcasses.

⁹ *"These you may eat of all that are in the waters: you may eat all that have fins and scales.* ¹⁰ *And whatever does not have fins and scales you shall not eat; it is unclean for you.*

¹¹ *"All clean birds you may eat.* ¹² *But these you shall not eat: the eagle, the vulture, the buzzard,* ¹³ *the red kite, the falcon, and the kite after their kinds;* ¹⁴ *every raven after its kind;* ¹⁵ *the ostrich, the short-eared owl, the sea gull, and the hawk after their kinds;* ¹⁶ *the little owl, the screech owl, the white owl,* ¹⁷ *the jackdaw, the carrion vulture, the fisher owl,* ¹⁸ *the stork, the heron after its kind, and the hoopoe and the bat.* ¹⁹ *"Also every creeping thing that flies is unclean for you; they shall not be eaten.* ²⁰ *"You may eat all clean birds.* ²¹ *"You shall not eat anything that dies of itself; you may give it to the alien who is within your gates, that he may eat it, or you may sell it to a foreigner; for you are a holy people to the Lord your God. You shall not boil a young goat in its mother's milk.*

Below, I have attached a table with a list of clean and unclean animals, to facilitate interpretation of the

verses described in Leviticus and Deuteronomy, regarding animals that we find nowadays, and thus to
better understand which ones we should eat if we do
not choose to be vegetarians:

Type	Clean	Unclean
a. Animals with four legs	Cow, deer, goat, ox, sheep *Ruminant with cloven-hoof	Camel, cat, rabbit, hare, dog, fox, bear, pig, mouse, horse, opossum, rat, rhino, squirrel
b. Birds	Goose, chicken, duck, dove, hen, turkey	Bat, raven, eagle, falcon, owl, pelican, ostrich, gull, hawk, vulture, stork, heron
c. Fish and species of animals that live in the sea and rivers	Salmon, grouper, tuna, herrings, cod, gold fish, flounder, largemouth bass, bass	Cat fish, clams, crab, eel, lobster, octopus, oysters, porcupine, shrimps, squid, stingray

| **d.** Insects | Grasshoppers, locust and crickets only

*Winged insects that walk on four legs, which has legs as well as to jump over them on ground. | The rest of the insects

*Winged insects that walk on four legs only, is abomination. |
| --- | --- | --- |

We are now clear about what is and is not good for us, according to the Word of God, regarding the meat of animals. Later, I will explain how good their advantages are.

All this is designed by God for us to live better, healthier, and to prepare our character in order for us to be saved for the second coming of our Lord Jesus Christ.

Physical habits have a lot to do with the success of every individual. Our physical health is maintained by what we eat; if our appetites are not under the control of a sanctified mind, and if we are not temperate in everything we eat and drink, then we will not be in a healthy mental and physical state to study the Word of God in order to learn what is said in the Scriptures (Ellen G. White, *Consejos sobre el*

Régimen Alimenticio, 60-61—In English: *Counsels on Diet and Foods*).

Something else that is vital, especially when going to put food in our body, is prayer: "If the Saviour of men, despite His divine strength, needed to pray," then how much more do we need it!? "When Christ was besieged by temptation, He didn't eat." In other words, He fasted. He surrendered to God, and by His fervent prayer and His perfect submission to the will of God, His Father, He was victorious (Ellen G. White, *Consejos sobre el Régimen Alimenticio, 61*—In English: *Counsels on Diet and Foods*).

Joel 2:12 – *"Now, therefore,"* says the Lord, *"Turn to Me with all your heart, with fasting, with weeping, and with mourning."*

With all this, we can see that we need to feed ourselves properly, according to His principles, which He wrote through His prophets in biblical times, to make us well in everything and to not become sick, but if by some neglection in obedience and temperance of these laws, we collapsed in any disease, we must stay strong and heal ourselves, preferably without drugs or medications, God's way.

6

The food in biblical times and what may

have been eaten by our Lord Jesus

Since the creation by God, man was omnivorous, meaning that man can live on both plant and animal based foods. But it has been demonstrated that the human body's design is best suited to the consumption of vegetables according to physical anatomy, primarily from their digestive system.

The food consumed in biblical times by obedience to the Word of God, and even more the foods that our Lord Jesus probably ate were:

1. **Bread.**

   King David ate bread regularly. Bread is mentioned many times in the Bible, and wheat and barley were the major grains eaten by the people of those times. There are others such as rice, corn, and oats. These were not consumed in the time of Jesus in Israel. Others mentioned in the Bible are millet and rye.

Ezequiel 4:9 - *"Also take for yourself wheat, barley, beans, lentils, millet, and spelt; put them into one vessel, and make bread of them for yourself. During the number of days that you lie on your side, three hundred and ninety days, you shall eat it.*

Mathew 6:9-13 - *9 In this manner, therefore, pray: Our Father in heaven, hallowed be Your name. 10 Your kingdom come. Your will be done on earth as it is in heaven. 11 Give us this day our daily bread.12 And forgive us our debts, as we forgive our debtors. 13 And do not lead us into temptation, but deliver us from the evil one. For Yours is the kingdom and the power and the glory forever. Amen.*

1 Samuel 25:18 - *Then Abigail made haste and took two hundred loaves of bread, two skins of wine, five sheep* *already dressed, five seahs of roasted grain, one hundred clusters of raisins, and two hundred cakes of figs, and loaded them on donkeys.*

Psalms 37:25 - *I have been young, and now am old; yet I have not seen the righteous forsaken, nor his descendants begging bread.*

2 Samuel 17:28-29 - *28 brought beds and basins, earthen vessels and wheat, barley and flour, parched grain and beans, lentils and parched seeds, 29 honey and curds, sheep and cheese of the herd, for David and the people who were with him to eat. For they said, "The people are hungry and weary and thirsty in the wilderness."*

I think that at that time the preparation of bread was very simple: the dough would have been made of wheat or corn with fresh water and sometimes, some seasonings to enhance the flavor, and its cooking on a flat stone on wood and fire, with the dough in the form of circular loaves, as Arabs today call pitas. Many times, I use cassava, a flour made from yucca that is very simple in flavor but high in fiber, as bread. It is similar to pitas in shape and the cooking is similar to this, on a stone, but the dough preparation is very complicated. Very commonly, in Venezuela, my country of origin and in other countries like Dominican Republic, it is prepared by the native (indigenous) in those regions. I eat, and also recommend Einkorn wheat. Besides being considered the oldest, it is original; in other words, its composition is not crossed (not hybrid), and it may have been the most similar to, or even consumed in biblical times. It is much healthier compared to the wheat consumed today in the world because of its very low gluten content, and simply for being the most pure and nutritious.

1 Corinthians 11:23-24 - [23] *For I received from the Lord that which I also delivered to you: that the Lord Jesus on the same night in which He was betrayed took bread;* [24] *and when He had given thanks, He broke it and said, "Take, eat; this is My body which is broken for you; do this in remembrance of Me".*

Jesus and His disciples ate wheat in its natural state.

Lucas 6:1 - *Now it happened on the second Sabbath after the first that He went through the grainfields. And His disciples plucked the heads of grain and ate them, rubbing them in their hands.*

Scrubbing wheat heads consisted of pulling off the shell, and leaving the more nutritious part: the bran and wheat germ. The wheat germ is rich in vitamin B, iron, magnesium, zinc, chromium, manganese, and Vitamin E. Wheat bran is also high in fiber.

The grain of wheat in biblical times was eaten roasted, boiled, mashed, and even naturally green from the tang. They ground, crushed, and dried the grain to eat it in soups, creams, salads with beans, stews, and in desserts.

There are also other forms, such as bulgur, which is used to make a popular salad among Arabs in the East called Tabule. Another one is the Couscus.

As for barley, nowadays, the one called "pearl" should not be eaten, because in this way, it is processed.

The use of wheat flour, or other grains to make bread and other foods, like cakes, was very common and consumed safely in biblical times, which today is not recommended because the nutrient properties of wheat have been altered with chemical procedures to produce flours. They are also blanched, and highly contaminated crops with pesticides, among other substances. The high gluten content, which is the protein found in grains and that can produce allergies, changes in the metabolism and in human hormones, causing diseases, but it is very popular because it is the component that gives the attractive flexibility to dough mainly as the wheat flour.

Modern baked breads (made of wheat flour) sold in bakeries and those packaged and sold at super markets, such as the ones for making sandwiches, are toxic to our bodies due to the chemical process in their preparation, in addition to the "strange" ingredients added to the process. Also, they use synthetic oils like canola, vegetable, corn, and soybean oil, among others that become rancid in our body and therefore are not healthy at all.

Some grains with little or no gluten content are: quinoa, millet, and amaranth.

Another way to consume the nutrients in grains is through their sprouts or herbs, such as wheat grass and barley grass. Both are rich in chlorophyll, the green blood of the plant and the equivalent of the hemoglobin in our blood, which carries oxygen. These are rich in flavonoids that are fotonutrients. Flavonoids have demonstrated to have anti-inflammatory, antiviral, and anti-tumor properties.

2. *Vegetables & Legumes*
Such as: peas, lentils, chickpeas that in biblical times were made in soups, purees,

and breads due to the fact that they can be dried and stored easily. I particularly prepare burgers for the kids and family with lentils, black beans, and chickpeas, but their best form as nutrients and protection from diseases is germinated. Nowhere in the Bible are soybeans named, so apparently it wasn't consumed in biblical times. Soybeans, especially consumed by vegetarians in recent decades has been considered super healthy food by them, but that is a big mistake!

Until recently, I made this mistake for years believing that soybeans could replace meats, cheeses, and milk from animals. We used to eat processed soybeans, such as in tofu and in almost everything, on our way to become vegetarians, which I now regret because the truth is that despite that it is coming from a grain or bean, it is one of the most genetically modified foods. Soybeans in the United States really became primarily a business. Soybeans have a high content of natural toxins, or anti-nutrients, and also produce pancreatic and thyroid problems, and eventually cancer. They contain a variety of ingredients, and their effects, which would not end in this book.

The funny thing is that they were not used in biblical times, and it was never recommended by God anywhere in the Bible.

> **Ezequiel 4:9** *Also take for yourself wheat, barley, beans, lentils, millet, and spelt; put them into one vessel, and make bread of them for yourself. During the number of days that you lie on your side, three hundred and ninety days, you shall eat it.*

The healthiest way to prepare beans, is by putting them to soak the night before, draining out the water the next day, and cooking them briefly, because by overcooking them, they lose their nutrient properties. The fresher, the better, since the cooking is faster.

A good meal with non-genetically modified whole grains and beans is rich in proteins.

Garlic, onions, and leek are beneficial both in medicine and nutrition. Garlic has antiseptic, antibacterial, antifungal, and antiviral properties; a few garlic cloves can reduce hypertension, and thus reduce the risk of a heart attack, among others. Onions are rich in Vitamins B and C. Besides that, they make for delicious seasoning to meals.

Cruciferous, such as broccoli, cauliflower, cabbage, collard greens, kale, watercress, and radishes among others, are widely recommended to reduce the risk of cancer.

Carotenoids are characterized by their color and their antioxidant power, which have been linked to great preventive properties against cancer of the colon, rectum, stomach, esophagus, prostate, breast, and possibly in other parts of the body.

Carotenoids have a pigment that gives a typically orange, yellow, and red color to lots of fruits and vegetables, such as oranges, carrots, and squash. However, we must clarify that this compound is also present in other green or dark green leaves like spinach or broccoli. Among them:

a) Beta-carotene is one of the essential nutrients that can be found in fruits and vegetables, also essential for maintaining good health. This is because it turns into Vitamin A in the body, which is a strong stimulant to the immune system.

Let us see some of the properties of beta-carotene, and their health benefits:

- It is a precursor of vitamin A (an essential vitamin to maintain our vision, skin, mucous membranes, and bones in good condition). When beta-carotene is ingested, it is tranformed into vitamin A.
- It is an excellent antioxidant, like vitamin E and C, and helps prevent cell aging and reduces the effect of free radicals in the body.
- Stimulates the immune system by strengthening the body's natural defenses. Favors the production of white blood cells.
- It is beneficial for the skin, as it also activates melanin, a natural protection against harmful sun rays. On the other hand, it is also known for its tanning action.

It is known to help us tan faster, however, always remember to be careful when tanning in the sun.

- There is also evidence suggesting that this compound is useful for preventing the onset of heart disease because it also provides protection against oxidative damage related to the "bad" cholesterol in blood.

- It is also associated with lowering the risk of developing certain cancers. It also protects the eyes from cataracts and prevents dry eyes.

- In the case of suffering from stomach ulcers, it also helps to reduce them thanks to its protective action on the stomach cells.

b) Lycopene is found in foods that are characterized with a red pigment, including: tomatoes, watermelon, pink grapefruit, pumpkins, sweet potatoes, apricots, and carrots. It is considered to have anti-prostate cancer properties.

c) Lutein is found in spinach, romaine lettuce, and kale (curly green cabbage) among others.

A person should consume these carotenoids daily for best protection and nutrition.

Foods rich in chlorophyll, which produce the green pigments in plants, have antioxidant properties and are also anticancerous. Among chlorophyll-rich foods are: spinach, parsley, and cilantro.

Vegetables and fruits are good sources of fiber. The high content of fiber in these foods helps lower cholesterol levels, stabilize blood sugar, and a number of other properties in the digestive system. Once in the intestinal tract, fiber helps combine toxins and expel them from the body before they are absorbed and can cause damage to cells and tissues.

Another food among the best vegetables are beets, a food we should not do without. It is a very energetic vegetable that is recommended in cases of anemia, blood disease, and a convalescent sick person due to its high iron content. It is also rich in sugars, vitamins C and B, potassium, and carotenes. The sugar in beets is sucrose.

Beets are particularly rich in folate. We have found that folate acid and folic acid prevent birth defects of the neural tube (nervous) and help against heart disease and anemia. Beets are also high in soluble and insoluble fiber. Insoluble fiber helps keep your intestinal tract working well, while soluble fiber keeps your levels of blood sugar and cholesterol controlled. It is one of the richest vegetable sugars. It contains folate and certain B vitamins, such as B1, B2, B3, and B6. By contrast, beets, along with eggplant or cucumber, are one of the vegetables with lower content of provitamin A and vitamin C. Folate is involved in the production of red and white cells in the synthesis of genetic material and in the formation of antibodies in the immune system. Regarding minerals, it is a vegetable rich in iodine, sodium, and potassium. Present in smaller amounts are magnesium, phosphorus, and calcium. Beta-carotene and minerals, such as iron and calcium, are abundant in its leaves.

Iodine, usually contained in salt for seasoning, is a prerequisite for proper functioning of the thyroid gland, which regulates metabolism mineral, while potassium and sodium are necessary for the generation and transmission of nerve impulses, activity muscle, in addition to intervening in the water balance inside and outside the cell.

To season food in biblical times, herbs and spices were used to give the foods more flavor, and also for medicinal purposes. Among them are cilantro, mint, and parsley.

Other seasonings, although not specifically mentioned in the Bible, but very good for their healing properties, antioxidants, for their ability to detoxify, for being anti-inflamatory, and their nutrients are: cinnamon, turmeric, saffron, ginger, mustard, and salt, preferably Celtic, Alaskan, or pink from the Himalayan Mountains (Nepal, China, or India). These condiments are generally minimally processed.

3. **Fish**
   In biblical times, fishing was very popular and the largest industry of that time. The Lord Jesus must have consumed fish according to what was recommended by God, His Father. They were most likely not contaminated, unlike nowadays.

Matthew 15:32-37 - [32] *Now Jesus called His disciples to Himself and said, "I have compassion on the multitude, because they have now continued with Me three days and have nothing to eat. And I do not want to* *send them away hungry, lest they faint on the way." [33] Then His disciples said to Him, "Where could we get enough bread in the wilderness to fill such a great multitude?" [34] Jesus said to them, "How many loaves do you have?" And they said, "Seven, and a few little fish." [35] So He commanded the multitude to sit down on the ground. [36] And He took the seven loaves and the fish and gave thanks, broke them and gave them to His disciples; and the disciples gave to the multitude. [37] So they all ate and were filled, and they took up seven large baskets full of the fragments that were left.*

Because mollusks and shellfish do not have scales, we should not consume them because they are unclean animals according to the Bible. Shellfish have the unique ability to purify water from bacteria such as cholera and salmonella. Toxins remain in the meat of the shellfish even though they are filters of water. Shellfish are the cockroaches of the sea, collectors of viruses, bacteria, parasites, and toxic waste. The Bible says they are an abomination to humans.

Leviticus 11:9-12 - *[9] 'These you may eat of all that are in the water: whatever in the water has* *fins and scales, whether in the seas or in the rivers—that you may eat. [10] But all in the seas or in the rivers that do not have fins and scales, all that move in the water or any living thing which is in the water, they are an abomination to you. [11] They shall be an abomination to you; you shall not eat their flesh, but you shall regard their carcasses as an abomination. [12] Whatever in the water does not have fins or scales—that shall be an abomination to you.*

4. **Fat** (Healthy vs. Harmful):

There is a myth among most people that all fats are bad, but this is not true.

Healthy fats are: olive oil, avocados, nuts, seeds, coconuts, and fats that come from animals raised naturally, such as fresh wild fish and grass-fed beef. The butter (saturated fat) from cows raised on grass is better than eating margarine (trans fat). For hundreds of years, many cultures around the world have consumed it without risk of heart disease. It contains conjugated linoleic acid, which is vital to the functioning of the brain and fat metabolism. These fats provide nutrients to your body required for cells' membranes to absorb vitamins, reduce inflammation, protect vital organs, maintain regulated hormones, and are the preferred energy source for your body. To repair the body's hormones due to an imbalance, healthy fats are needed.

Harmful fats are fats that are altered in the process of removing it from its original source. Besides being unhealthy on the cellular level, these are:

- Hydrogenated oils (trans fats), which were designed to preserve the life of packaged food and other products on the shelves of markets.
- Vegetable oils, which the process comprises chemical extraction using extracts of solvents. Among these oils are: soybean, corn, canola (this oil has nothing natural; it is rapeseed genetically manipulated by man to reduce its toxic acids; the name "CANOLA" actually comes from "Canadian Oil Low Acid" for its acronym in English), safflower, and cottonseed among others.

The food that I highly recommend should be eaten fresh, raw, or undercooked and whole, preferably organic and non-genetically modified (Non-GMO) without the use of genetic engineering, which means they are not contaminated and processed for altering their genetics and causing rapid growth, especially if you live in the United States. This recommendation is costly to our pockets, but worth it because what could be more expensive is a visit to the doctor or even a hospital.

The typical American diet was not the way our Lord Jesus Christ and people in biblical times ate. Obviously, in biblical times, none of this happened. It's amazing that in almost a century of America being the healthiest nation, it has become the most deteriorated in health, and all of this, for some groups, is to make more money, prepararing the famous fast foods, so that we get sicker rapidly, and at the same time, supporting the pharmaceutical companies and hospitals. The problem with these kinds of ambitious groups is the way they are processing these foods that have been killing thousands of people; but they are profound socio-economic issues that I will not discuss this book.

Finally, I believe that we must not exaggerate or be extremists and fall into fanaticism at all; not much of the bad, and neither short of the good. We must have a balance in everything. If we cannot find or cook what we know is good for our health and we are far from the reach of the products that we consider healthy, then I recommend a proportion of 90-10%, 90% being the healthy products and 10% being what is not good. My advice is to not always eat the same thing, considering that God in His mercy to us, His children, created a huge variety of fruits and vegetable because some good things, in excess, can be toxic, so everything should be eaten with variety and in moderation.

In prayer and thanksgiving, we will bless our food that we are going to eat, and God will hallow it for us, even those things that man has damaged, like genetically modified fruits and vegetables.

1 Timothy 4:4-5 - *[4] For every creature of God is good, and nothing is to be refused if it is received with thanksgiving; [5] for it is sanctified by the word of God and prayer.*

Something more I want to add, is that everything you buy in the markets, you must read the labels. Packaged food products that have obviously been processed, contain many ingredients, and ingredients you can not read or understand on the label. There is a very popular phrase these days that says: "If you cannot read it, do not eat it." This means that if you cannot read or understand the ingredient used in the process as an end product because of the complicated chemical terminology added to its content, then you should not eat it because it means that it is synthetic. In other words, it is obtained by industrial processes, usually chemical synthesis, which reproduces the composition and properties of some natural bodies; in other words, it is not real, nor pure, nor natural.

In all these recent years, a variety of topics related to health and lifestyle have been released, so there is lots of information, but there are also contradictions, especially due to the increasing population of overweight people because we are all in the search of the purest and most beneficial foods and products to consume and bring to the table for our families every day in the middle of a highly polluted and toxic world. At the time I wrote this book, this was the most accurate information I researched. It has worked for me as I said earlier, and it is consistent in accordance with the Bible.

7

My recipes and menus for the week

To cook good and healthy food with fresh ingredients, you do not need anything fancy or sophisticated equipment to prepare it, just a little creativity and of course appetite!

Breakfast, as its name suggests, is "after the fast," so you can not skip it. In the morning, your metabolism has to turn on, so it is necessary to break the fast. Unless you are doing a spiritual fast to pray and meditate with God, otherwise, whether you'll go to work or take the children to school, we must have breakfast, remembering to take care of the temple of the Holy Spirit that is sacred.

In this chapter, I want to share some of my recipes, quick and easy, for those who live very busy lives like me, and for those who do not as well.

I use organic fruits and vegetables especially with my meals. Also, for the rest of the ingredients, I prefer to use, especially if you live in the United States, non-GMO (not genetically modified), and if I am going to add cheese, butter, eggs, or any meat, like chicken or turkey, in other words, any products derived from animals to the foods, then use those from farms where animals are raised outdoors (cage free) and grass-fed, with the grass not contaminated with pesticides (organic). And if you are going to eat fish, the recommended fish should be wild, taken directly from the sea, but preferably the seas of Northern Alaska, like the salmon is, though the purity of the fish is doubtful in any sea or ocean in this world. The fish in the world are heavily contaminated by radiation and toxic waste thrown into the sea. Nowadays, fish should be consumed rather moderately.

Another recommendation, since our stomachs need rest between meals, is that we should wait at least 5 hours for the next meal.

Also, I want to clarify that mixing fruits with vegetables has been a controversial topic, but what I know so far is that it is not good for people that have a weak digestive system. If this is the case, the person has to eat only fruits or vegetables in separate meals and not mixed together.

Now, onto some of my favorites recipes. I hope you will try, and enjoy them!

Breakfast

Smoothie #1:
(4 servings)

- 1 banana
- ½ cup of black cherries
- ½ cup of blackberries
- ½ cup of blueberries
- ½ cup of strawberries
- ½ cup of almonds
- 1 whole lime (preferably with skin)
- 1 piece of ginger
- 1 piece of turmeric
- 1 green apple
- 2 big leaves of kale with its stems
- ½ beet
- 2 carrots
- Water

Put everything in a blender, preferably in one of high potency, such as the Vitamix. Every morning, during the week, my children, my husband and I drink a smoothie for breakfast similar to this depending on the ingredients (fruits and vegetables always) I have available at home. Always add greens. If you don't find or have kale, you can add spinach, broccoli, preferibly the stems, celery, and/or sprouts of any kind. I prefer to use broccoli sprouts or alfalfa. You can also stir in chia seeds. A tip for when you add the whole lime (with the skin), is that the smoothie must be drunk immediately because it will become bitter soon. To avoid this, you can just add the lime juice as another alternative or option. In this case, the lime juice should be double the portion. If you don't have almonds or walnuts, which is the protein, then you can use oats, maybe about ½ cup soaked in water overnight.

Smoothie #2:
(3 servings)

- 10 oz/284 gr. black cherries
- ¾ cup shredded coconut (or Coconut flakes)
- 1 tbsp turmeric (powder)
- 2 tbsp hemp seeds
- 2 cups spinach leaves
- 2 carrots
- ½ big beet
- ¾ cup walnuts
- 1 whole lime or the juice of 1 lime
- Water

The preparation for all my smoothies is the same: mix or blend all ingredients, and drink one of the best gifts given to us by God from mother nature according to His principles of health and healing.

Smoothie #3:
(3 servings)

- 3 kale leaves
- 4 kiwis
- 2 bananas (small)
- 3 tbsp hemp seeds
- 1 piece of ginger
- ½ cup of almonds
- 1 lime
- Coconut milk (13.5 Fl.Oz./398 ml.)
- 10 oz/284 gr. blueberries
- 2 carrots
- ½ red beet
- 1 tsp cinnamon (or to taste)
- Water

Same as the other smoothie recipes: put everything in a blender and enjoy a rich and nutritious breakfast. I add water even if I am using coconut milk, because this combination of the coconut milk with blueberries curdles the preparation very quickly, so if this happens, you can eat it as a yogurt.

Pancakes (or Waffles):
(4 servings)

- ½ cup Einkorn flour or coconut flour
- 1 egg
- 1 tbsp of sugar from the cocunut palm or honey
- Applesauce
- Coconut oil (to fry)
- Water

Mix all the ingredients by hand with a spatula and put ¼ cup of the mixture in a skillet or a waffle maker with a teaspoon of coconut oil and fry each pancake or waffle. Once the pancake or waffle is golden brown and cooked, which may be in about 5-10 minutes, then you can use butter, jam, honey, or grade B maple syrup on top, which is one of the best and healthiest syrups. You can eat it alone or with fruits, depending on the taste you wish to achieve.

Cereal:
(1 serving)

In a bowl:

- Sliced bananas (and/or papaya)
- Shredded coconut
- Raw Goji Berries (Himalayan berries)
- Homemade Granola (Oat flakes, cranberries, raw cane sugar, quinoa, orange oil or orange shavings, Kosher salt [Kosher means that it has not been in contact with animal blood and clean of it in the case that it was])
- Orange or lime juice
- Turmeric & cinnamon powder

You can make variations of this recipe. I also like it with ½ cup of coconut milk, cinnamon powder, and adding ¼ cup of ground almonds or walnuts.

Lunch

Cole Slaw:

(4 servings)

- ½ green cabbage
- ½ purple cabbage
- ¼ red onion
- 4 radishes
- 2 carrots
- 1 red beet
- Salt to taste
- Juice of a lime
- 1 tbsp of honey or Maple syrup
- Organic, non-GMO mayonnaise

Put cabbage, onion, radishes, carrots, and beet in a food processor, cut them in small pieces, or simply shred them. Then add the remaining condiments. I like to put this salad on top of a tortilla or a slice of sprouted bread (grain and gluten free) with an avocado.

Black Bean Burgers:
(8 servings)

- 1 ½ cups of cooked black beans
- ½ cup of cooked quinoa
- ½ cup red onion
- ½ cup bread crumbs or P.A.N. (Venezuelan) corn flour
- 2 eggs
- ½ cup cilantro
- 2 garlic cloves
- 1 red pepper
- Adobo spices to taste (if desired)
- Salt to taste
- Coconut oil (to fry)

Mix all ingredients except for the bread crumbs in a food processor, make 2-inch diameter cakes, batter them with the bread crumbs or flour, and then fry them in coconut oil, and then they are ready to eat! They are delicious! You can make them with different types of beans and have them with a side of cole slaw on a bed of spinach and ¼ avocado.

Spaghetti Squash:
(4 servings)

- 1 spaghetti squash
- 12 asparagus
- 1 cup of mushrooms
- 1 tbsp of butter
- 1 package (4 oz./113 gr.) Goat cheese
- Salt to taste

Put the spaghetti squash in the oven at 350°F for 1 hour. Then take it out and wait until it is cold to shred with your hands taking apart the strips. Then, put them in a saucepan or frypan and sauté them with butter, salt, and asparragus cut in pieces. At the end, put the cheese crumbs.

Dinner

Broccoli Cream Soup
(8servings)

- 1 cluster of broccoli with stems
- 1 leek
- 1 zucchini
- ½ red pepper
- 1 ginger piece
- 1 tbsp salt
- 1 tbsp of Extra virgin coconut oil
- 1 tbsp Turmeric
- ½ cup Cilantro
- 2 garlic cloves

Put all ingredients (except cilantro, turmeric, and ginger) in a saucepan, preferably of glass, with water. Once it has boiled, turn off and leave to rest until cool, then is when you put the cilantro, turmeric, and ginger, and blend it.

<u>Squash Cream Soup:</u>
(4 servings)

- 2 butternut squashes
- 1 carrot
- 1 can (13.5 oz) coconut milk
- 1 red pepper
- ¼ cup cilantro
- 1 tsp turmeric
- 2 tbsp extra virgin olive oil
- Salt (to taste)

Put 2 squash in the oven at 350°F, and once they are tender take them out and peel them. Then blend in a Vitamix with a carrot, coconut milk, turmeric, salt, cilantro, red pepper, and extra virgin olive oil. If you do not have a Vitamix, then heat the soup in a glass saucepan.

Zucchini and Squash Casserole and Mac & Cheese made of Cauliflower:
(2 servings)

- 2 zucchinis
- 1 yellow squash
- 1 tbsp grassfed butter
- 2 cups mozzarella or havarty cheese
- 1 head cauliflower
- 2 cans (14 oz) hearts of palm
- 10 cherry tomatoes
- 1 cup spinach
- 1 cup almond flour
- Salt (to taste)
- Extra virgin olive oil (to taste)
- Fig balsamic (to taste)

Cut 2 zucchinis and a squash and sautée in butter for 10-12 minutes, then add 1 tablespoon of butter, 1 cup of almond flour, and 1 cup of mozzarella, or havarty shredded cheese onto the zucchini and squash, and broil in the oven until golden. Next, put a head of cauliflower in boiled water and salt for short time, then rinse it and cut in little pieces and add the hearts of palm the remaining cheese to make the grainless, vegetarian version, without pasta of *"macaroni and cheese."* Pair with a side of a tomato and spinach salad with extra virgin olive oil and fig balsamic.

Eggplants, Yucca and Caprese Salad:
(4 servings)

- 1 eggplant
- 2 eggs
- Breads crumbs
- 2 roots of Yucca
- 2 cups of Spinach
- 2 tomatoes
- Basil leaves
- Extra virgin olive oil
- Salt

The eggplant, in slices, need to be dehydrated first with salt to remove the excess water. This has to be made for 24 hours, then fry the previously slightly breaded eggplants in coconut oil. With this procedure, you can make a lasagna, or an eggplant parmesan, with napolitan sauce (tomato sauce), and mozzarella cheese on top, and in layers then broil it in the oven, as another option for dinner, this dish is quick and easy. Put the roots of yucca in boiled water with salt until tender and you can add butter and set on a bed of spinach leaves or with a cilantro dressing made with garlic and red sweet pepper.   The caprese salad is made with tomato slices, mozarella cheese, basil leaves on top, salt to taste, and lastly, extra virgin olive oil.

Chocolate cake (Gluten free):
(12 Servings)

- 1 ½ cups of cooked black beans
- 5 eggs
- 1 tsp of vanilla essence
- ½ cup of Coconut palm sugar
- 6 tsbp of butter or coconut oil
- 6 tbsp cocoa powder without sugar
- 1 tsp of Baking powder (Aluminum free)
- ½ tsp Baking soda
- 1 tbsp of water

Preheat the oven to 325°F, drain the beans, free of any residual water, and put them in the blender with 3 eggs, and the sugar. Blend until everything is well mixed or liquid without lumps. Then, with a hand mixer, put cocoa, baking powder, and baking soda in. Then, add the butter with the remaining 2 eggs until the mix is soft. Put the mix in a pan in the oven for 40 minutes.

These are a sample of the many recipes I have been creating God's way, from a recipe book that I will be publishing in the future.

I hope you have enjoyed this guide and the informative reading content in this book that, with love and for the glory of God, I wanted to share with you all, my family, friends, and all brothers and sisters in Jesus Christ, who want to know more about God, Who is the same as yesterday and today, and Who wishes in His immense love for us, that we stay healthy, happy, and prosperous.

References

- Holy Bible – New King James Version (NKJV)
- Dodie Osteen. (1986). *Healed of Cancer.*
- Don Colbert, MD. (2012). *La Nueva Cura Bíblica Para la Depresión y Ansiedad.* Casa Creación.
- Don Colbert, MD. (2003). *¿Qué comería Jesús?* Grupo Nelson.
- Don Colbert, MD. (2006). *The Seven Pillars of Health.* Siloam.
- Mark Finley. (1991). *Estudiando Juntos - Manual de Referencia Bíblica.* Hart.
- Max Lucado. (2014). *Sobre el Yunque.* Casa Creación/Editorial Nivel.
- Ellen G. White. (2008). *Consejos sobre el Régimen Alimenticio.* Asociacion Publicadora Interamericana.

- Maximized Living, Dr. BJ Hardick, Kimberly Roberto, and New York Times Best Selling Author Dr. Ben Lerner. (2009). *The Solution of the Dangers of Modern Nutrition "Nutrition Plans."* Maximized Living.

About The Author

Brigida Tellez, is a Civil engineer graduated in Venezuela, South America, with a major in Structures, however, for many years, from the time God blessed her with her children, has been working as a Spanish-English interpreter and translator, and as a technical support of educational projects at the County where she lives with her husband, her children, and her dog close to Atlanta, Georgia in the USA. Also, she is studying in an University for a Master of Arts in Teaching Foreign Languages major in Spanish and for a certification.

At churches where she has been a member, she helps with translations, writes for devotionals, as well as elaborates presentations and newsletters, supports the women's ministries, presents lectures and radio programs on health and nutrition, and in the kitchen, she prepares healthy recipes.

One of her favorite things to do is walking, typically several miles or running outdoors. She enjoys cooking and always creating new dishes "God's way." She also likes going to the beach, sharing with her family and friends, and visiting her family in Venezuela. She helps others as much as possible. Her dedication to write and share the love of God will continue until Jesus Christ returns for the second time to this world.

53027410R00065

Made in the USA
Charleston, SC
03 March 2016